Meet Robby the C-130

Beth Mahoney

ILLUSTRATED BY
Zachary Porter

ISBN-13: 978-1441456595 ISBN-10: 1441456597

Dedicated to my children;
Robby, Alex, and Rachel
for being such wonderful little helpers
every time daddy was deployed.

www.robbythec130.com

www.RobbytheC130.com

This is Robby. Robby is a C-130 airplane. Robby's job is to help the military. He carries supplies and soldiers all over the world.

Robby is a very big and strong airplane. He can carry many things. He can even carry a utility helicopter and armored vehicles with six wheels.

Robby has so much to do that he has five friends to help him; two pilots, a navigator, a flight engineer, and a loadmaster.

The two pilots help Robby fly and help him land safely. They sit in the very front so they can see everything Robby sees. The pilots are like Robby's glasses, they help him see better and further!

The navigator tells Robby which way to go and how to get to where they are going. He tells Robby which way to turn and how far to go.

The Flight Engineer makes sure Robby stays healthy while he is flying. He is like an airplane doctor that monitors Robby's fuel, air conditioning, and electrical systems.

The Loadmaster makes sure everything that Robby is carrying with them is safely secure and balanced. He helps Robby load and unload the supplies or soldiers.

Sometimes Robby has to go away from home for a while to bring the supplies and soldiers to many different places.

Robby is always sad when he has to leave home and he misses his family, but Robby has a job to do and the soldiers really need him to help.

When Robby is away from home, he works very hard to keep the soldiers and supplies moving. Robby works different hours during the day and night.

Sometimes when they are not working, he loves to listen to his friends tell jokes, play games, and read to him. He is glad he has friends with him when he is away from his family.

Other times Robby gets sad and cries when he is alone because he misses his family. Do you get sad or cry when your mommy or daddy is away from you?

To help pass the time, Robby tries to play games and make fun crafts while he is apart from his family. What do you do to help pass the time and cheer yourself up?

Robby loves to get letters, pictures, and videos from his family back home. It cheers him up! Do you write letters and take pictures for your mommy or daddy when you are apart?

When it is time for Robby to go back home, he loves to see all the banners and American Flags that everyone decorates to welcome him home. But most of all, Robby loves to see his family again!

The End

Can you draw a picture of your parents?

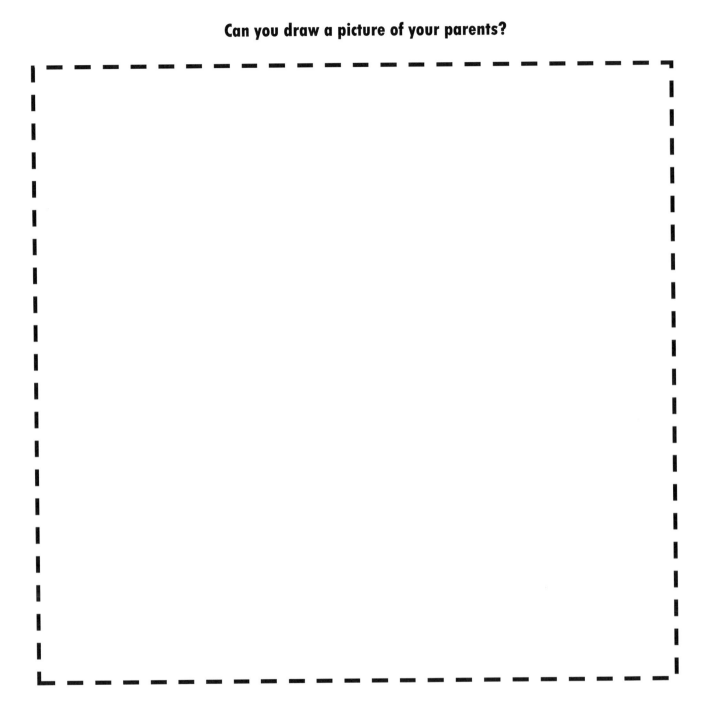

How do you feel when your mommy or daddy goes away?

What do you want to do when your mommy or daddy returns?

How do you feel when your mommy or daddy returns?

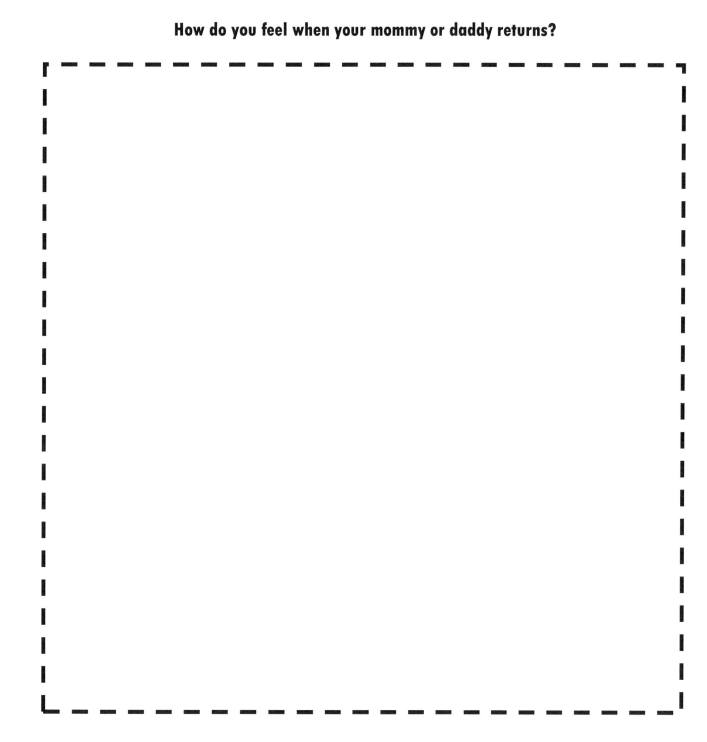

Draw a picture of your whole family together!

Write a letter to your mommy or daddy!

Dear _____,

_____

_____

_____

_____

_____

_____

_____

Love,

_____

For Parents: 5 Ways to use this book

1 Discuss with your child the many emotions she has built up inside. Let her know it is ok to feel the way she does and that it makes us feel better when we cry, just like Robby does when he is feeling sad.

2 Ask your child what activities she would like to accomplish while your spouse is deployed. Robby likes to play games and craft, so she might have similar interests.

3 Have your child use the drawing spaces to draw out or vent her frustrations in color. Let her explain to you what she is drawing and why.

4 Help your child write a letter to your spouse and cut it out to send as soon as possible. Let her cut out the other pictures if she wants or take photographs and/or videos to send along.

5 Use the resources enclosed to help you and your children cope with the deployment.

Military Children's Resources

Military Child Education Coalition (MCEC)

http://www.militarychild.org/

MCEC is a 501(c)(3) non-profit, world-wide organization that identifies the challenges that face the highly mobile military child, increases awareness of these challenges in military and educational communities, and initiates and implements programs to meet the challenges.

Operation: Military Kids (OMK)

http://www.operationmilitarykids.org/public/home.aspx

The U.S. Army's collaborative effort with 4H and America's communities to support the children and youth of National Guard and Army Reserve Soldiers impacted by the Global War on Terrorism.

Robby the C-130

http://www.robbythec130.com

The official website of Robby the C-130 and friends. Visit Robby online to see pictures, videos, and download activities.

National Military Family Association (NMFA)

http://www.nmfa.org/

"The Voice for Military Families," is dedicated to providing information to and representing the interests of family members of the uniformed services. Providing information on deployment, education, family life and health care, and resources.

About the Author

Mrs. Mahoney is an Author, Editorial Photo Journalist and Content Writer for geek parenting, video games, technology, and military blogs and publications, and speaker for digital parenting and military families. Currently she is the Editor Chief, Community Director and Internet Radio Talk Show Hostess for a moms community which focuses on educating and informing parents, women, and mothers in the digital age, technology, and video game industry as well as including books and publications for and about children, parents, and families.

Since 2008 she's been publishing children & family books with a focus on military family support. She Founded a non-profit organization for military children, that works closely with military officials, school Principals, and Counselors to provide better communication between schools and military families. She was a guest speaker for Arkansas Governor Beebe on military family issues, was a featured Children's Author at the Arkansas Literary Festival, and she was a guest Author at Lockheed Martin, home of the military aircraft. Mrs. Mahoney was also award 2009 LRAFB Volunteer of the Quarter, was the founding committee chair for Month of the Military Child, and nominated National 2010 Military Spouse of the Year by CINCHouse and Military.com.

Aside from her professional life, Mrs. Mahoney is a proud military spouse and geek mom to three brilliant nerds, two of which are Autistic. She enjoys creative minds, positive people, photography, and the Mass Effect video game! She also likes to go by her middle name, Kat, and she has two dogs named Dexter (Jack Russell Terrier) and Zeus (Boxer). Email Mrs. Mahoney at bmahoney@robbythec130.com and visit www.robbythec130.com

**Look for more Robby C-130
at www.RobbytheC130.com**

37449152R00020

Made in the USA
Lexington, KY
02 December 2014